WORKBOOK

FOR

The

Gifts Of

Imperfection

LET GO OF WHO YOU THINK YOU ARE

SUPPOSED TO BE AND EMBRACE WHO YOU ARE

By

BRENÉ BROWN

WONDER BOOKS

Table of Contents

How To Use This Workbook

The goal of this workbook is to help you realize that you have the ability to make changes, choices and decisions that will help you grow and live a wholehearted life.

This only happens when you answer the questions from each chapter genuinely. Answering the questions will not only make you stop to pause and think but it will also make you become deliberate and intentional with your everyday life.

At the beginning of each chapter/guideposts are important lessons to bring salient points to your fingertips.

The goal is for you to make the best out of life and to be able to offer this to your children as you can only give what you have. So relax, carry out the exercises given to you and practice a wholehearted life.

INTRODUCTION

This book helps you to make meaningful living out of life and this is the essence of wholehearted living. It will bring awareness and clarity to the constellation of choices and principles that lead to Wholeheartedness.

The principles in this book have been tested and trusted to lead you to loving yourself and worthiness instead of chasing after perfection. This is why it is important to understand courage, compassion and connection and most of all, practice them to gain worthiness. The first chapter takes an in-depth look into these three concepts.

The second chapter talks about love, belonging and worthiness, three things important to the soul of anyone who lives. The third chapter looks into things that get in the way of wholehearted living and the guideposts are filled with practices to provide direction for your life and journey.

Each concept has been defined and the digging deep posts are all about DIG: becoming **D**eliberate, getting **I**nspired and **G**oing (taking action).

Who Should Read This?

This book is for everyone who desires to live a wholehearted life which is a life that is balanced, joyful and beautiful.

Life comes with lemons and no one is perfect but as we begin to practice Wholeheartedness our lives becomes better and we attract the right kind of people.

What's In It for Me and Why Is It Important?

When you read and **practice** what you learn from this book, you'll find out that your life becomes easier.

This doesn't mean the challenges of life become easier but it simply means you are better prepared for the challenges and you can rise above any challenge. You can smile from deep within you and at the end of your life, you have no regrets.

You will soon discover:

- You aren't alone in all that you feel or experience
- You can become better
- There's more to you than you know if only you let yourself grow and experience true spirituality
- Wholeheartedness is possible
- Love especially self-love is way better than shame
- While trying to fit-in you lose yourself
- Play and rest are essential and unbeatable
- Laugh, dance and sing as much as you can

Courage, Compassion and Connection: The Gifts of Imperfection

Here are some key points we learned in this chapter:

- Practicing courage, compassion and connection daily will lead to a life of worthiness.

- Courage only comes by getting involved in courageous acts just as we become compassionate by extending compassion to ourselves and others. Our ability to connect with others comes from our ability to reach out to others and connect with them.

- You don't need to go out of your way to win people over. Doing this may lead to you stepping out of the principles to please others. It is also known as trading authenticity for approval.

- Shame only thrives and grows in the dark. Bring the story to the light. Speak out! The twin companion of shame is fear.

- When looking for the right person to share your story with, make sure the person is flexible, deeply rooted and can accept you no matter your mistakes, weaknesses and struggles.

- Shame and fear don't stand a chance against acceptability and love.

- The pristine meaning of courage means to speak one's mind by telling all one's heart; so speaking honestly and being vulnerable about who we are, how we feel and what we are going through is courage.

- To be compassionate, you need to know how to relax and face your fears. Compassion is Latin in origin and it means 'to suffer with'.

- Compassion can only happen between equals not a healer and wounded. Only when we understand our darkness and shortcoming can we relate with the darkness of others. It's impossible to be compassionate without acceptance.

- To hold people accountable and be compassionate, bring in consequence for their actions where necessary and separate people from their behavior

- Connection is the energy that exists between people when they feel that they are heard, seen and valued or when they feel they can give or receive judgment. These people derive the strength they need from such relationships. It brings fulfillment and satisfactions to both parties.
- Technology doesn't mean people connect. Let go of the myth of self-sufficiency. No man was made to go through life alone.

Answer the following questions as sincerely as you can

1. Without practice, it's impossible to cultivate anything meaningful

   True [ ]

   False [ ]

2. Wholeheartedness requires courage

   Yes [ ]

   No [ ]

3. Do you believe courage is only about being heroic?

   Yes [ ]

   No [ ]

4. You can't gain courage without doing things that require courage

   True [ ]

   False [ ]

5. Can life be meaningful without courage, compassion and connection?

Yes [ ]

No [ ]

6. Compassion makes us kinder but firmer

True [ ]

False [ ]

7. Our first response to pain is to protect ourselves which is why we try to shield ourselves by blaming others or trying to fix-it.

True [ ]

False [ ]

8. Does everyone deserve a right to hear your story?

Yes [ ]

No [ ]

9. To get over shame, share the story that led to shame

True [ ]

False [ ]

10. Do you have something you're secretly ashamed of?

Yes [ ]

No [ ]

i.   Write out the event

_____

_____

_____

_____

_____

_____

_____

ii.   How do you feel now that you've let it out?

_____

_____

_____

_____

_____

_____

11. Have you ever shared your story with anyone and it was a disaster as the story was everywhere?

Yes [ ]

No [ ]

12. Have you ever shared your story with anyone and it led to connection, compassion and you've been close ever since?

Yes [ ]

No [ ]

13. Which of the following would you want from someone you're sharing your story with?

Someone who feels the shame you feel   [ ]

Someone who is horrified   [ ]

Someone who sympathizes   [ ]

Someone who empathizes   [ ]

Someone who replies with clichés (bless your heart)   [ ]

Someone who is disappointed in you   [ ]

Someone who can be vulnerable   [ ]

Someone who sees you as a perfect person and role model   [ ]

Someone who scolds you   [ ]

Someone who can't listen and always interjects   [ ]

Someone who wants to fix you   [ ]

14. Have you ever tried to forcefully right a wrong or make someone believe in you and it seemed like you were losing faith in yourself?

Yes [ ]

No [ ]

15. What happened?

_____
_____
_____
_____
_____
_____
_____

16. How did you manage or get over the situation?

_____
_____
_____
_____
_____

17. Which of these 'right' work with compassion?

Right person   [ ]

Right balance   [ ]

Right words   [ ]

Right mindset   [ ]

Right timing   [ ]

Right issue   [ ]

Right attitude   [ ]

Right thinking   [ ]

Right experience   [ ]

18. To be totally exposed or vulnerable, accepted and love can be described as _____.

19. Tick the box that best describe courage?

Heartfelt response   [ ]

Honestly   [ ]

Vulnerability with another   [ ]

Heroism   [ ]

Ordinary courage   [ ]

Risking disappointment over everything   [ ]

20. Why did you tick the box you did? Can you link it to any experience you've had?

_____

_____

_____

_____

_____

_____

_____

21. Lack of courage leads to

Isolation   [ ]

Anxiety   [ ]

 Guilt   [ ]

Overexcitement   [ ]

Mixed feelings   [ ]

Depression   [ ]

The inability to connect with others when it's important   [ ]

Becoming judgmental   [ ]

To be compassionate you need to   [ ]

Get over your fears   [ ]

Get over the fear of setting boundaries and holding people accountable[ ]

Get over your judgmental attitude   [ ]

Walk through your mistakes   [ ]

Be kind   [ ]

22. Is it possible to be kind on the outside but anger, bitter, judgmental and resentful on the outside?

Yes [ ]

No [ ]

23. Is it possible to be compassionate without setting boundaries and holding people accountable for their behavior?

Yes [ ]

No [ ]

i. Why did you choose your answer? Can you describe an event or scenario that best explains the reason for your answer?

_____

_____

_____

_____

_____

_____

_____

24. Have you tried to hold people accountable by shaming or blaming them or has someone done it to you?

Yes [ ]

No [ ]

i. How did it feel?

_____

_____

_____

_____

_____

_____

_____

25. If you are a teacher and you have students who don't like to participate or do their assignments, what's the best way to show compassion when managing such situation?

_____
_____
_____
_____
_____
_____
_____

26. Mention the people with whom you share a deep sense of connection

_____
_____
_____
_____
_____
_____
_____

27. Look at the first person on your list and mention how you got to share a deep connection with the person.

_____
_____
_____
_____
_____
_____
_____

28. Did courage and compassion help you share a connection with the person?

Yes [ ]

No [ ]

i.   If yes, how? If no, why not?

_____

_____

_____

_____

_____

_____

_____

29. Have you ever felt you were deeply connected with someone but later found out you weren't? How did you find out?

_____

_____

_____

_____

_____

_____

_____

30. Is there a difference between giving help and receiving help? Is one higher?

Yes [ ]

No [ ]

i.   Explain your reason

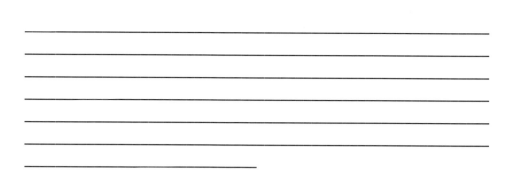

Exploring the Power of Love, Belonging and Being Enough

Here are a few points we learned in this chapter

- The difference between those who have a sense of love and belonging and those who don't is the struggle for it and their belief in their worthiness. To enjoy and experience love and belonging, you must first know that you're worthy of it. Without this knowledge, you'll fight for it.
- When we let go of what other people think and own our story we become worthy of the love and belonging we worked so hard to gain. Our sense of worthiness, love and belonging lies in our story.
- You're worthy of love not when you meet all conditions but right now. Try to gain a better understanding of what love and belonging mean.
- Don't try to fit in, just belong. The two aren't the same thing.
- Love and belonging happen within an indefinable space that we may never fully understand. Love and belonging go together. They are like right and left hands or leg working together. A deep sense of love and belonging is an irreducible need of all women, men and children.
- Everyone has an innate ability to love as long as we are all human. It's a biological, cognitive, physical and spiritual feeling every human has.
- Learn to practice self-love. It makes you trust yourself, be kind to yourself, treat yourself with respect and do the same to others.
- Cultivating self-love and self-acceptance isn't optional. It is the prerequisite to loving others.

Answer the following questions as sincerely as you can

1. Shame and love can't be taken away from vulnerability and tenderness

True [ ]

False [ ]

2. Fitting in gets in the way of belonging

True [ ]

False [ ]

3. Love and belonging will always be uncertain and non-essential to all humans

True [ ]

False [ ]

4. Have you ever been disappointed and ashamed because of what other people think about you?

Yes [ ]

No [ ]

i. Did you get over it?

Yes [ ]

No [ ]

ii. If you did, how did you feel afterwards?

_____

_____

_____

_____

_____

_____

_____

5. Are there parts of your life you secretly wish didn't exist?

Yes [ ]

No [ ]

i.   If your answer is yes, why?

You hate that part   [ ]

It demeans you   [ ]

It makes you disappointed in yourself   [ ]

It takes you back to your past   [ ]

It reminds you of how flawed you are   [ ]

You don't want anyone to know that part of you   [ ]

It feels you with so much shame   [ ]

No one would come close to you if they knew   [ ]

6. Have you felt you had to meet up with certain requirements in order to feel worthy of love and belonging?

Yes [ ]

No [ ]

i.   Can you write out some of those requirements? Is it looking good, losing weight or buying a new car? Write them out.

_____

_____

_____

_____

_____

ii.   Were you ever able to meet up with these requirements?

Yes [ ]

No [ ]

7. What does love mean to you?

_____

_____

_____

_____

_____

_____

_____

8. Tick the right boxes

Love is something we give or get   [ ]

Love is just a feeling that springs up   [ ]

Shame, disrespect, betrayal and love have the same roots   [ ]

We can only love when we give ourselves to love   [ ]

Belonging makes you to be part of something bigger than you   [ ]

Belonging is an answer to a yearning   [ ]

Belonging is not part of our DNA   [ ]

We can either allow or disallow belonging   [ ]

Without belonging, life isn't worth living   [ ]

Belonging makes us gain approval from others   [ ]

True belonging comes from vulnerability and showing ourselves to the world   [ ]

Our sense of belonging must be higher than our level of self-acceptance   [ ]

9. You have a teenage daughter who is smitten by a boy in her class and she believes she loves him. However, he doesn't notice her and it hurts her. Help her understand the uncertainty of love and belonging.

_____

_____

_____

_____

_____

_____

_____

10. As a teacher, you have a student who was seen as a geek and a nerd, he had good grades but he has no friends. You suddenly notice he has a group of friends he moves with but his grades drop. What is he trying to do?

Fit in [ ]

Belong [ ]

i.   How can you help him understand the difference between the two

_____

_____

_____

_____

_____

_____

_____

11. Do you think love is essential for every human?

Yes [ ]

No [ ]

12. Tick the right boxes

Without love and belonging we

Hurt   [ ]

Become happy   [ ]

Grow and develop   [ ]

Go numb   [ ]

Ache   [ ]

Become broken   [ ]

Live normal lives   [ ]

Die   [ ]

Become sick   [ ]

Suffer   [ ]

13. Have you ever found it easier to forgive someone for the wrong they did than to forgive yourself even when you did the same thing?

Yes [ ]

No [ ]

i.   Why so? Do you feel you were too silly to make such a mistake? Write down your reason.

_____

_____

_____

_____

_____

_____

_____

ii.   Can loving yourself be a remedy?

Yes [ ]

No [ ]

iii.   Why so?

_____

_____

_____

_____

_____

_____

14. Mention 3 people you love the most and you tell them you love them

_____

_____

_____

15. Recall the times where you were really mean to them

_____

_____

_____

_____

_____

_____

_____

16. Does your action to them and what you profess (saying I love you) really match or do you take them for granted because you love them and you expect that they should understand?

_____

_____

_____

_____

_____

_____

_____

The Things That Get in the Way

Here are some points we learned in this chapter

- Be real and honest in every way. Never let your fears get in the way. Bring it out in the open and you'll realize that the anxiety drops.
- To move forward, you will need to be vulnerable enough to speak up about the things you can't do.
- Sometimes using a list on how to get things done may not work for you. Know what makes you distinct and stick with it.
- Maintaining your focus in the midst of shame, fear and chaos as we gaze upon the other side of the swamp where all that's good and makes us worthy waits for us is more difficult than even trying to cross to the other side. Shame, fear and our present status would do all to make us stay where we are.
- When we struggle to believe our worthiness, we hustle for it. It's yours already so own it.
- Shame is universal. Don't believe you're the only one who goes through it. Those who don't go through it either block away the feelings or they lack the ability for empathy and human connection.
- Shame has no power in the light. The more you hide it, the stronger it becomes.
- If someone tries to define you by your story and makes you feel ashamed or full of fear, know that you need to keep your gaze on who you're becoming.
- We can develop shame resilience. It's the ability to recognize shame, move through it constructively without losing authenticity, worthiness so you become courageous, compassionate and you can connect with others out of your experience. Shame resilience can sneak up on you without you knowing.
- There's a difference between shame and guilt. An individual who feels guilty can separate their actions from their person while the one who feels shame can't separate the two. Shame says I'm

terrible while guilt says I acted terribly. Guilt can lead to a positive effect while shame is out rightly destructive.

Answer the following questions as sincerely as you can

1. To feel shame is to be human

   True [ ]

   False [ ]

2. Shame loves perfection

   True [ ]

   False [ ]

3. Shame can sneak up on you without your knowledge

   True [ ]

   False [ ]

4. Make a list of the most embarrassing things that happened to you that caused you shame and fear

   _____
   _____
   _____
   _____
   _____
   _____
   _____

   i. Mention one of these most embarrassing experiences you've ever had that you've kept to yourself over the years

   _____
   _____
   _____

_____

_____

_____

_____

    ii.   Why are you keeping it to yourself?

_____

_____

_____

_____

_____

_____

    iii.   What's the worst that can happen if those you're truly connected with find out?

_____

_____

_____

_____

_____

_____

_____

    iv.   What do you need to face that fear and deal with it?

_____

_____

_____

_____

_____

_____

_____

5. What are the things people think you can do but you can't?

_____

_____

_____

_____

_____

_____

_____

6. Your daughter came back home from school and told you of how she was embarrassed and ashamed because she gave a poor performance at a presentation in school. She doesn't want to go back to school again. How do you help her wade through it or get over it?

_____

_____

_____

_____

_____

_____

_____

7. Here are things that stand in my way to becoming a better me

Anxiety   [ ]

Fear   [ ]

Shame   [ ]

Feelings of unbelief   [ ]

Doubt   [ ]

Too much pressure I put on myself   [ ]

What people think   [ ]

I don't love myself   [ ]

My past   [ ]

I can't fit in   [ ]

I'm not good enough   [ ]

Comparing myself to others   [ ]

Disappointing others   [ ]

i.   Imagine you have a son or a group of teenagers who have these same challenges. How can you help them get over it?

_____

_____

_____

_____

_____

_____

_____

8. Have you been scared of connecting with someone because you felt if they heard your story they will never recover?

Yes [ ]

No [ ]

9. When you spoke with the person and you noticed they were compassionate and you connected with them, how did you feel?

_____

_____

_____

_____

_____

10. Which of the following does shame need to grow?

Secrecy   [ ]

Simplicity   [ ]

Judgment   [ ]

Jokes   [ ]

Silence   [ ]

Trust   [ ]

Anger   [ ]

11. Tick the boxes that applies to people who has shame resilience

They understand shame and they can identify what triggers it for them[ ]

They know imperfect doesn't mean inadequate   [ ]

They identify people they can connect with and share experiences with them   [ ]

They don't shy away from the word shame   [ ]

They don't hide or suppress how they feel   [ ]

They know how to ask for help   [ ]

They don't judge others   [ ]

They are strict with others and stricter with themselves   [ ]

12. Have you ever experienced shame without knowing? How did you find out and get over it?

_____

_____

_____

_____

_____

_____

_____

13. Has someone ever shamed you publicly and you immediately responded from shame resilience and not shame?

Yes [ ]

No [ ]

i.   What happened and how did you handle it?

_____

_____

_____

_____

_____

_____

_____

14. How do you manage when nasty words are hurled at you and you're tempted to please people?

_____

_____

_____

_____

_____

_____

_____

15. Have you ever felt hurt or small at work or among friends and family as a result of what someone said to you?

Yes [ ]

No [ ]

i.   What was the most courageous thing you did at that time?

_____

_____

_____

_____

_____

_____

_____

GUIDEPOST #1
Cultivating Authenticity: LETTING GO OF WHAT PEOPLE THINK

Here are a few points we learned

- Many people have a misguided definition of authenticity. It's not a characteristic we have or don't have; rather it's an intentional choice of the way we choose to live or a combination of choices we make daily that has determined who we are.
- It's letting go of who we think we are while embracing who we are meant to be.
- Being authentic or staying real is a battle and not just any kind of battle, it's a courageous battle. Everyone around you or those who love you may be in the way of your reality or they may say you're changing too much.
- We need to have the audacity of authenticity. Without it, you may not be able to differentiate self-indulgence from shame triggers.
- As you struggle or dare to be authentic and brave, don't expect everyone to be on your side. Some people will criticize you, some will be cruel and say all sorts of things because they are threatened and they love the notion they have always had about you.
- The best gift you can give to yourself and others you love is to be true to yourself.

Answer the following questions as sincerely as you can

1. Sacrificing yourself for what others think, feel or know about you isn't worth it.

True [ ]

False [ ]

2. To be authentic, you must get deliberate, get inspired and get going.

True [ ]

False [ ]

3. Tick the following boxes that describes what authenticity means to you

It's a choice   [ ]

It's an option   [ ]

It's a reality that you project   [ ]

It describes who you are   [ ]

It fosters courage, compassion, connection and sense of belonging[ ]

It's a combination of the choices you make everyday   [ ]

It's something you choose when things are convenient   [ ]

It's your decision to live honestly   [ ]

Its intentional living   [ ]

It's the way you make decisions   [ ]

It's a consciousness   [ ]

4. Has there ever been a time when you made good decisions that made you joyful but you were too scared to feel the joy because you felt you were not good enough for joy to happen to you?

Yes [ ]

No [ ]

i.   Why?

_____

_____

_____

_____

_____

_____

_____

5. Have you ever found it hard to love yourself?

Yes [ ]

No [ ]

6. Do you weigh all the good things you do and compare it to all the bad things you do to decide if you are good enough to be loved?

Yes [ ]

No [ ]

7. Do you feel good things in life aren't real or they don't last where you're concerned?

Yes [ ]

No [ ]

i.   Why?

_____

_____

_____

_____

_____

_____

_____

8. You have a little nephew who has poor grades at school and he doesn't get too close to people because he's afraid they will know he has poor grades and he will behave poorly among them. What do you think the problem is?

_____
_____
_____
_____
_____
_____
_____

i. How can you help him or guide him? What can you tell him?

_____
_____
_____
_____
_____
_____
_____

9. Has there ever been a time where you had to stay real and true to your choices even when it was difficult?

Yes [ ]

No [ ]

i.   Was everyone around you against your decision?

Yes [ ]

No [ ]

ii.   What happened and how did you manage the situation?

_____

_____

_____

_____

_____

_____

_____

10. Is it difficult for you to be authentic?

Yes [ ]

No [ ]

i.   Why is it difficult for you to be authentic?

The idea of perfection everyone has about me will crumble   [ ]

I know I'm not enough or good enough   [ ]

Others must know that I'm not enough   [ ]

If everyone sees my imperfection, they'll hate me   [ ]

I always want people around me   [ ]

My world may crumble   [ ]

It wouldn't make me fit in or belong   [ ]

I don't want people to be uncomfortable   [ ]

I don't want to hurt people because I know how it feels   [ ]

I don't want it to seem like I'm the know it all   [ ]

I want peace no matter the cost   [ ]

I want to feel safe   [ ]

It doesn't match up with what society and culture approves   [ ]

11. Was there a time you had to negotiate between showing your true self to the world and risking what everyone things or says or the criticisms?

Yes [ ]

No [ ]

i. How did you feel when you gave in to everything except your authenticity?

Rage   [ ]

Anger   [ ]

Lack of peace [ ]

Resentment   [ ]

Bitterness   [ ]

Addictions   [ ]

Depression   [ ]

Insomnia   [ ]

Sadness   [ ]

    ii.   Write out the other things you felt?

_____

_____

_____

_____

_____

_____

_____

    iii.   How did you get over it?

_____

_____

_____

_____

_____

_____

_____

    iv.   Were you able to forgive yourself afterwards?

Yes [ ]

No [ ]

12. Tick the following boxes that describe how you can stay authentic and true to yourself and others in any situation

Be deliberate when you're in a vulnerable situation   [ ]

Understand what you're staying true to   [ ]

Don't see yourself as too small or not enough   [ ]

Smile always and seek people's counsel   [ ]

Be brave and daring   [ ]

Read wide   [ ]

Get information and knowledge that can keep you inspired   [ ]

Stay aloof   [ ]

Exercise more   [ ]

Make authenticity your goal   [ ]

Love yourself   [ ]

Never allow yourself become vulnerable   [ ]

Look past shame, fear and guilt   [ ]

Understand your flaws   [ ]

Make authenticity your priority   [ ]

GUIDEPOST #2
Cultivating Self-Compassion:
LETTING GO OF PERFECTIONISM

Here are a few things we learned

- If you think you don't have a problem with shame but you are a perfectionist then you have a problem with shame. Shame is the foundation for perfectionism. If you don't claim shame it will claim you. The way to shame is perfectionism.
- Perfectionism makes you follow rules and please people. With perfectionism, you are the same as your actions and you are all about performance.
- There's a difference between healthy striving and perfectionism. You must be able to differentiate between the two to experience wholehearted living. Perfectionism will always lead to anxiety, addiction, depression and other health challenges.
- Perfectionism leads to life-paralysis. Life-paralysis is a term that describes missed opportunities due to the fear of failing, imperfection, mistakes and disappointing others.
- Perfectionism is self-destructive and addictive. Its main goal is perfection for the purpose of preventing shame, judgment and blame.
- It's all about the perception of perfection. This is why perfectionists experience shame, blame and judgment as there's no way to control people's perception.
- Perfectionism leads to more perfectionism because it doesn't question the faulty logic of perfectionism but rather focuses on how to look, live and do everything just right.
- Embrace your imperfections. That's the way to find your truest gift.
- Perfectionism never happens in a vacuum. We pass it down to our children, our colleagues, friends and families and we suffocate them with it. This is the same way compassion happens. When we

are compassionate with ourselves, we also spread it to our children, friends, family and workplace. This is how we can truly be free, authentic and connected.

Answer the following questions as sincerely as you can

1. Shame and perfectionism are related

    True [ ]

    False [ ]

2. Shame is for those who claim it

    True [ ]

    False [ ]

3. Perfectionism leads to life-paralysis

    True [ ]

    False [ ]

4. Feeling judged, blamed and shamed is a normal part of the human life

    Yes [ ]

    No [ ]

5. Tick the boxes that describe perfectionism

Perfectionism is striving to be your best   [ ]

Perfectionism means healthy growth, development and achievement [ ]

Perfectionism is a way to deal with blame   [ ]

Perfectionism is learning and acting perfect   [ ]

Perfectionism is living above guilt, shame and judgment   [ ]

Perfectionism is a weight that drags you down   [ ]

Perfectionism grants you opportunities   [ ]

Perfectionism makes you want to gain approval and fit in   [ ]

Perfectionism encourages success   [ ]

6. Take the perfectionism test

i.   Have you ever tried to prove to people that you're the best by doing so much to please them?

Yes [ ]

No [ ]

ii.   Do you like pleasing people?

Yes [ ]

No [ ]

iii. Are you more bothered about what people think than how you can improve?

Yes [ ]

No [ ]

iv.   Do you believe in meeting all the requirements before you get a promotion

Yes [ ]

No [ ]

v.   Do you think it is wrong to take instinctive decisions instead of following the steps to get an opportunity?

Yes [ ]

No [ ]

vi.   Did you grow up in a house where the best child was the one who got the highest praise because they obeyed all instructions?

Yes [ ]

No [ ]

vii.   Were you constantly compared with other kids who had the best grades?

Yes [ ]

No [ ]

viii.   Do you put up an acceptable behavior or say the right things in front of everyone even if that's not what you truly feel?

Yes [ ]

No [ ]

ix.   Would you do everything and anything to prevent criticism?

Yes [ ]

No [ ]

x.   Do you feel terrible within yourself when you don't get things right?

Yes [ ]

No [ ]

xi.   Do you believe everything must be right without a fault?

Yes [ ]

No [ ]

xii.   Do you accept, regard, disregard and judge people based on what you see?

Yes [ ]

No [ ]

xiii.   Have you ever stopped yourself from giving your best because of all the things that could go wrong?

Yes [ ]

No [ ]

(If most of your answers are yes then you have both perfectionism and shame.)

7. Your see your son and ask him about his science fair project. He tells you that he's pulled out of it because he's too scared that his plans might fall apart. How can you help him see that perfectionism isn't helpful?

_____
_____
_____
_____
_____
_____

_____

8. How do you help fifth-graders differentiate between healthy striving and perfectionism?

_____
_____
_____
_____
_____

9. Have you ever worked on a task years ago and tried to make sure everything was perfect but it didn't go the way you wanted it to go?

Yes [ ]

No [ ]

10. Does it still hurt that it wasn't perfect?

Yes [ ]

No [ ]

11. Do you think everyone still remembers what you did?

Yes [ ]

No [ ]

12. Have you ever been judgmental and critical about yourself? How do you prevent yourself from shame attacks and judgment that you instinctively subject yourself to?

_____
_____
_____
_____
_____
_____
_____

13. You met your neighbor's teenager look lost and depressed because she couldn't pass an exam and she says it's her fault because she's not brilliant enough. How do you help her become shame resilient and compassionate?

_____

_____

_____

_____

_____

_____

_____

14. Two major ways to overcome perfectionism include

_____

_____

_____

_____

15. Imagine you need to talk to a bunch of teenagers about how to overcome perfectionism. Write a story about how you've always been perfect, how you changed and how they can aim for healthy striving.

_____

_____

_____

_____

_____

_____

_____

16. Why is self-compassion essential when trying to deal with perfectionism?

_____

_____

_____

_____

_____

_____

_____

17. What are the three important elements of self-compassion?

_____

_____

_____

_____

GUIDEPOST #3
Cultivating a Resilient Spirit:
LETTING GO OF NUMBING AND POWERLESSNESS

Here are a few lessons we learned

- Deeply embedded in resilience are each individual's protective factors which are the things we do, have and practice to give us bounce. Our bounce is determined by our spirituality which every individual has.
- Spirituality is recognizing and celebrating that we are all connected by a power that's greater than us and the connection we share with that power is deeply rooted in compassion and love.
- By practicing spirituality, we gain a sense of perspective, direction, purpose and meaning in our lives. Without spirituality, there can be no resilience.
- The three patterns essential to spirituality are cultivating hope, practicing critical awareness, and letting go of numbing and taking the edge off vulnerability, discomfort and pain.
- When we know that we're inextricably connected, then we don't feel alone and that lifts the weight off our shoulders.
- Have you heard people say unless blood, sweat, tears, pain, toil and suffering isn't involved then it's not important? That's not true! However, if you're used to fast, fun and easy then you're going to be disappointed along the way. Hope is a balance of the two sides as it involves perseverance and flexibility.
- We need to practice critical awareness because it helps us check what we see or hear that makes us feel we aren't good enough.
- We all numb and take the edge off and this can get in the way of our authenticity. It can keep us from feeling connected and becoming vulnerable.

- Understanding behavior from a vulnerability lens is a better way to see than understanding behavior through an addiction lens.
- There's nothing called selective emotional numbing. Joy is as thorny and sharp as sadness, anger or pain. When we lose our tolerance for discomfort we lose our joy. Leaning into the discomfort of vulnerability makes us know how to live with joy, gratitude and grace.

Answer the following questions

1. Resilience helps you stay mindful and authentic under stress and anxiety

    True [ ]

    False [ ]

2. Resilience helps you transform trauma into Wholehearted thriving

    True [ ]

    False [ ]

3. Tolerance for disappointment, determination and a belief are at the heart of hope

    True [ ]

    False [ ]

4. If you numb your pain, you numb your joy

    True [ ]

    False [ ]

5. What does spirituality mean to you? Is it connecting to God, the universe, yourself or allowing yourself absorb the positivity around you? Explain it.

_____

_____

_____

_____

_____

_____

_____

6. Do you think practicing spirituality can bring you healing and help you create resilience?

Yes [ ]

No [ ]

7. Tick the boxes that best describe resilient people

They are resourceful   [ ]

They are amiable   [ ]

They are peaceful   [ ]

They have good problem-solving skills   [ ]

They would rather give help than receive help   [ ]

They believe in doing something that can help them manage their emotions   [ ]

They can't control their nerves   [ ]

They have a good support system   [ ]

They are courageous and share a good connection with others   [ ]

8. You have a student who has a dream of becoming a baseball star but he has a fractured limb and lost his father. However, he's beginning to give up on his dream. How do you help him find and learn hope?

_____

_____

_____

_____

_____

_____

_____

9. Tick the right boxes that clearly describes hope to you

Hope is nothing more than a feeling or emotions   [ ]

Hope can be learned   [ ]

Hope depends on you believing in yourself   [ ]

Hope makes you have a sense of entitlement   [ ]

Without flexibility, hope can be unattainable   [ ]

Realistic goals and instinct is what helps you when you need hope [ ]

Hope can either be an instinctive choice or a conscious choice   [ ]

Hope needs persistence and hard work to thrive   [ ]

Hopelessness is as powerful as hope   [ ]

10. Your niece comes to your house for the holidays. You notice she wants everything to be fun, super-fast and with no sweat involved. Create a task to teach her how to persevere and hope.

_____

_____

_____

_____

_____

_____

_____

11. At the end of the day before you sleep, go over your day. Pay attention to all that happened all throughout the day especially the things you saw before you answer the following questions.

i.   Do all the things I saw today work in the real world?

Yes [ ]

No [ ]

ii.   Does it represent wholehearted living or will it make me objectify everything?

Yes [ ]

No [ ]

iii.   What did I gain from seeing these things?

_____
_____
_____
_____
_____
_____
_____

12. Your daughter watched a fashion show and she wanted to be a model ever since. She has stopped eating well due to this. How can you help her?

_____
_____
_____
_____
_____
_____
_____

13. Have you ever tried to stop the pain or hurt or any emotion you're feeling?

Yes [ ]

No [ ]

i.   How did you do it?

Getting busy   [ ]

Making or spending money   [ ]

Pouring yourself into work   [ ]

Shopping   [ ]

Sex   [ ]

Drugs   [ ]

Sugar addiction   [ ]

Alcohol   [ ]

Relationships   [ ]

Perfectionism   [ ]

Eating   [ ]

Incessant worrying   [ ]

Depression   [ ]

Doing something new   [ ]

Surfing the internet   [ ]

Planning   [ ]

Gambling   [ ]

ii.   Mention others

_____
_____
_____
_____
_____
_____
_____

iii.   Why do you do it?

_____
_____
_____
_____
_____
_____
_____

iv.   Does this stop you from becoming emotionally honest and vulnerable?

Yes [ ]

No [ ]

v.   Are you scared of getting emotionally honest and vulnerable?

Yes [ ]

No [ ]

vi.   Why?

_____
_____
_____
_____
_____

_____

_____

14. Write out your daily spirituality routine and practice it. After two weeks, check to see if you notice any difference in your life.

GUIDEPOST #4
Cultivating Gratitude and Joy: LETTING GO OF SCARCITY AND FEAR OF THE DARK

Here are some of the points we learned

- You don't need to fit in but to belong. To feel a true sense of belonging requires baring yourself out and bringing the real you to the table. This can only happen when you practice self-love.
- Gratitude is a practice and joy is a step beyond happiness. You can create an atmosphere for happiness when you're lucky. Happiness is attached to external situations and events and seems to ebb and flow as those circumstances come and go. Joy seems to be tethered to our hearts by spirit and gratitude.
- A joyful life is made up of joyful moments gracefully strung together by trust, gratitude, inspiration and faith.
- Until we tolerate vulnerability and transform it into gratitude, intense feelings of love will often bring up the fear of loss.
- If you're not practicing gratitude and you're not embracing joy, you'll miss out on the two things that can serve as your anchor when there are hard times.
- A mindset of sufficiency deals brings to light the mindset of lack (not enough). Sufficiency doesn't have anything to do with quantity or amount. It's an experience, a generated context, a declaration and knowing there is enough and we are enough.

Please answer the following questions

1. I must first experience and practice self-love before I can feel a true sense of belonging

True [ ]

False [ ]

2. Joyful people are grateful people because joy must come before gratitude

   True [ ]

   False [ ]

3. Sufficiency lies in each of us and we can call it forth

   True [ ]

   False [ ]

4. Gratitude without practice can positively affect your life

   Yes [ ]

   No [ ]

5. Does staying grateful and joyful mean you're always happy?

   Yes [ ]

   No [ ]

i.   Why? Do you think it means you always have to be in a good mood? Explain your reason.

_____

_____

_____

_____

_____

_____

_____

6. Think about your daily experiences. Is it possible to be constantly joyful or happy all of the time?

Yes [ ]

No [ ]

7. Tick the boxes that truly describe joy and gratitude

To live a joyful life, you must actively practice gratitude   [ ]

Joy and gratitude can't be divorced from spirituality, human interconnectedness and a power greater than us   [ ]

Happiness is the same emotion as joy.   [ ]

Joy is a spiritual way of engaging the world that's connected with practicing gratitude   [ ]

The basic foundation for joy is self-love   [ ]

Circumstances can take away your happiness but not your joy   [ ]

Gratitude is a practice that comes from making a habit out of an action [ ]

8. Vulnerability helps us embrace joy and gratitude

True [ ]

False [ ]

9. Do you have a daily gratitude routine?

Yes [ ]

No [ ]

10. What is your daily gratitude routine or attitude? Is it having a quiet time, keeping a gratitude journal, mindfulness, meditation or praying? Can you create one if you don't have one? Write it down

_____

_____

_____

_____

_____

_____

_____

11. From your experiences, would you say joy and happiness are two different things?

Yes [ ]

No [ ]

12. Using one of your recent experiences, explain the difference or similarities

_____

_____

_____

_____

_____

_____

_____

13. Can we live with either joy or happiness or do we need both? Why?

_____

_____

_____

_____

_____

_____

_____

14. Which of the following clearly explains the opposite of *chairo* (joy)?

Sadness   [ ]

Depression   [ ]

Fear   [ ]

15. Have anxiety and fear stood in the way of joy and gratitude for you?

Yes [ ]

No [ ]

i.   Why? Do you feel it's too good to be true, you're expecting something terrible to happen afterwards, it won't last or it's all happening too fast? Write down your reasons.

_____
_____
_____
_____
_____
_____
_____

16. You kind and sweet new neighbors will soon become new parents. You told them about embracing gratitude and joy and they broke down in tears out of fear. Tell them how embracing gratitude, vulnerability and joy can help them.

_____
_____
_____
_____
_____
_____
_____

17. Write out one of your greatest fears and your reason for the fear. Is it losing a child because she was playing on the road or going bankrupt because you lost all your money and you have no job? Write it out

_____

_____

_____

_____

_____

_____

_____

18. Now imagine you had a younger sibling who just got married and shared his thoughts on the same fear with you. How do you help him/her? Can you step out from the situation and look at it independently? Will you tell them it will never happen or tell them to embrace vulnerability and gratitude? What would you say or do? Write it down.

_____

_____

_____

_____

_____

_____

_____

19. Do you ever wake up in the morning and think of aspects of your life where you're not enough? Or do you do this before you sleep?

Yes [ ]

No [ ]

i.   What are those aspects? Is it your weight (I'm not thin enough), your looks (I'm not good-looking), is it your career (I'm not smart enough, successful enough or influential enough), is it money (I'm not rich enough)? Mention them

_____

_____

_____

_____

_____

_____

_____

ii.   Do you think a mindset of sufficiency can change the difference from the mindset of lack (not enough)?

Yes [ ]

No [ ]

iii.   Why? If your answer is yes, do you think it fill you with gratitude? If your answer is no, do you think nothing can change what you feel? Write down your reasons.

_____

_____

_____

_____

_____

_____

_____

20. Get a bunch of sticky notes. Write what you're grateful for on them and place them in places where you'll easily find and read them. It could be your bedside, your refrigerator or your closet door. Remind yourself of these whenever you feel overwhelmed.

21. Get a gratitude journal. It doesn't have to be a big book, a little journal or notepad would do. Write out what I'm trusting, what I'm grateful for, what inspires me and how I'm practicing my faith.

Write each one on separate pages. On the first page which is what I'm trusting, write out things you're trusting for; it could be a new job or a new apartment. On the next page which is what I'm grateful for; it could be being alive, being able to smile or any other thing. On the next page write out the things that inspire you; it could be your spirituality, your faith, family and friend. On the last page which is your faith, write out how you carry out what you're trusting, grateful for and what inspires you.

GUIDEPOST #5
Cultivating Intuition and Trusting Faith: LETTING GO OF THE NEED FOR CERTAINTY

Here are a few lessons we learned

- Intuition isn't a single way of knowing – it's our ability to hold space for uncertainty and our willingness to trust the many ways we've developed knowledge and insight, including instinct, experience, faith and reason.
- Faith is a place of mystery, where we find the courage to believe in what we cannot see and the strength to let go of our fear of uncertainty.
- If we learn to trust our intuition it can tell us that we don't have a good instinct on something and that we need more data.
- Intuition isn't always about access into the answers from within. Sometimes when we've tapped into our inner wisdom it tells us that we don't know enough to make a decision without more investigation.
- We need both faith and reason to make meaning in an uncertain world
- Faith is essential when we decide to live and love with our whole hearts in a world where most of us want assurances before we risk being vulnerable and hurt.
- Try going still deep within when you feel fear and anxiety taking over your instinct

Please answer the following questions

1. Intuition and faith work hand in hand

True [ ]

False [ ]

2. Intuition tells you what you need to know

    True [ ]

    False [ ]

3. Fear of the unknown and fear of being wrong creates most of our conflict and anxiety

    True [ ]

    False [ ]

4. To live a Wholehearted life requires that you believe even when you can't see or prove what you feel.

    True [ ]

    False [ ]

5. Would you rather look to others for assurances than follow intuition?

    Yes [ ]

    No [ ]

6. Have there been times when you discarded intuition for certainty?

    Yes [ ]

    No [ ]

i. Why did you do it? Was it because it makes you feel you're walking in the dark or it feels like your whole world would crumble or it feels like something could go wrong? Write down your reason

_____

_____

_____
_____
_____
_____
_____

7. Think of a particular experience you went through where you had to work with intuition and trust faith. Write it down

_____
_____
_____
_____
_____
_____
_____

    i.   How did you feel as you were going through this experience? Were you nervous, anxious or worried about what was going to happen eventually and what everyone was going to say? Write it down.

_____
_____
_____
_____
_____
_____
_____

    ii.   When things eventually worked out perfectly or close to perfectly, how did you feel? Exhilarated, joyful, happy, excited? Write it down

_____
_____

_____

_____

_____

_____

_____

8. Tick the boxes that aptly describe intuition

Intuition makes you shut down your mind   [ ]

Intuition makes you flexible and vulnerable   [ ]

Intuition works like magic   [ ]

Intuition works with the brain and gut   [ ]

Intuition makes sure you find the missing pieces of a puzzle [ ]

Intuition helps you pay attention   [ ]

Intuition helps you focus on your instinct   [ ]

9. Your child was given a step-by-step process in a project in school. He says his gut feels like he should make changes. What would you do or say to him? Will you teach him to gain more knowledge, carry out due diligence or would you tell him to stick to the rules? How can you help him?

_____

_____

_____

_____

_____

_____

_____

10. I don't trust my instinct because

It leads me to listen to my gut and I don't know how   [ ]

I can't walk alone   [ ]

It's easier to blame someone when things fall apart   [ ]

I'm trying to avoid mistakes   [ ]

I don't want to slow down   [ ]

I'm smart enough to think things through   [ ]

I don't want anything messing with the plans I made   [ ]

It stresses me out   [ ]

It leads me to due diligence which can be tiring   [ ]

11. How do you come to a place of faith when you need to make decisions and use your intuition? Give an example with an experience you've had.

_____

_____

_____

_____

_____

_____

_____

GUIDEPOST #6
Cultivating Creativity: LETTING GO OF COMPARISON

Here are a few things we learned

- Comparison is all about competition and conformity.
- When we compare we want to see who or what is best out of a specific collection of 'alike things'.
- The more entrenched and reactive we are about an issue, the more we need to investigate our responses.
- Creativity is the power to connect the seemingly unconnected.
- Everyone is creative. There's nothing like creative and non-creative people. There are only people who use their creativity and those who don't.
- The only unique contribution we will ever make in this world will be born of our creativity.
- As long as we're creating, we're cultivating meaning
- To let go of comparison, keep your eyes on yourself and not on what others are doing.

Please answer the following questions as sincerely as you can

1. Conforming and competing stand in the way of creativity

    True [ ]

    False [ ]

2. To make meaning make art

    True [ ]

    False [ ]

3. Conforming and competing are mutually exclusive

True [ ]

False [ ]

4. Constant awareness is the key to managing comparison

True [ ]

False [ ]

5. Have you ever compared yourself to anyone? Why did you compare yourself to the person?

_____

_____

_____

_____

_____

_____

_____

6. You took your kids out to buy some toys and they tell you they want something better than what their friends have. How do you help them stop comparison?

_____

_____

_____

_____

_____

_____

_____

7. Tick the right boxes that best describe what comparison does

Comparison does nothing but steal your happiness   [ ]

Comparison eats the soul   [ ]

Where comparison exists, people hate each other   [ ]

Comparison helps your creative abilities   [ ]

Comparison makes you fit in   [ ]

Comparison helps you gain a sense of belonging   [ ]

Without comparison, concepts like ahead, behind, best and worst are unnecessary   [ ]

8. Did you grow up comparing yourself with your friends or neighbors or did your parents compare you to others?

Yes [ ]

No [ ]

i.   How did it make you feel?

_____

_____

_____

_____

_____

_____

_____

ii.   Would you want your kids to grow up like that?

Yes [ ]

No [ ]

iii.   Did you get over it? If you did, how did you get over it?

_____

_____

_____

_____

_____

_____

_____

9. What are the most creative things you've done? Is it writing, cooking, sculpturing, playing with kids or thinking of great ideas? Mention them

_____

_____

_____

_____

_____

_____

_____

10. Do you believe everyone but you is creative? If you believe this why do you think so? Is it because you feel everyone is better than you or creativity is only for kids or everyone is competing with you? Write down you reasons.

_____

_____

_____

_____

_____

_____

_____

11. What was the most creative thing you did as a child and you enjoyed it so much?

_____

_____

_____

_____
_____
_____
_____

i.   Why did you enjoy it? Was it because it allowed you to be yourself or was it because there was no pressure? Write down your reasons.

_____
_____
_____
_____
_____
_____
_____

12. Think of something creative you can do. It doesn't have to fit into anyone's explanation. Think of something interesting and fun that you can do.

_____
_____
_____
_____
_____
_____

i.   If you think you can't do it, write out the reasons why you can't. Is it too childish, is it time consuming or too taxing or something happened when you were a child that made you stop or your parents complained? List out your reasons

_____
_____

_____

_____

_____

_____

_____

ii.   Now imagine that you told your child or protégé to come up with something creative and he brought up the same list of reasons you came up with. What would you say or do? Do you tell him to his reasons are valid or you help him to work through his reasons? What would you do? Write it out.

_____

_____

_____

_____

_____

_____

_____

13. Tick the right boxes that best describe creativity

Creativity helps to deal with feelings of shame and fear   [ ]

Creativity brings out the child in you   [ ]

Creativity is negative   [ ]

Not everyone has the ability to be creative   [ ]

When creativity isn't used it dies   [ ]

To be remarkable and outstanding you need to be creative   [ ]

Creativity is art and for people related to art not sciences   [ ]

You can choose to use your creativity   [ ]

Fear and resentment can kill creativity   [ ]

14. Take up something to inspire your creativity. It can be dance lessons, decorating classes, music lessons, sculpting, singing, acting, painting or taking pictures. Journal about your experiences and how it has made you improve. You can do this daily or weekly. At the end of the month or three months read about your experiences and how much you've improved and grown.

GUIDEPOST #7

Cultivating Play and Rest: LETTING GO OF EXHAUSTION AS A STATUS SYMBOL AND PRODUCTIVITY AS SELF-WORTH

Here are a few things we learned

- Play is essential to us all no matter our age. It is essential to our health and functioning as rest.
- Play is purposeless.
- There's a connection between the biological need for play and the body's need for rest
- To live wholehearted lives we have to become intentional about cultivating sleep and play and about letting go of exhaustion as a status symbol and productivity as self-worth.

Please answer the following questions as sincerely as you can

1. The opposite of play is depression

    True [ ]

    False [ ]

2. When it comes to work, play is essential as it can transform and uplift our work

    True [ ]

    False [ ]

3. Sleep debt is linked to diabetes, high blood pressure, depression, obesity and other heart diseases

True [ ]

False [ ]

4. Sleep is a luxury

True [ ]

False [ ]

5. Do you think busy and exhaustion should be a normal part of life?

Yes [ ]

No [ ]

6. Tick the boxes that explain what play does to humans

Play shapes the brain	[ ]
Play encourages empathy	[ ]
Play helps us relax	[ ]
With play comes courage, compassion and connection	[ ]
Play gives room for innovation and creativity	[ ]
Play helps us to socialize	[ ]
Play helps individuals find a sense of belonging	[ ]
Play leads to rest	[ ]
Play brings out the fun side of you	[ ]
Play re-energizes you	[ ]
Play helps us work creatively and excitedly	[ ]

7. Stay with your kids for four days. In the first two days, make sure they don't play and in the following two weeks, make sure you play with them. (If you can do this for 10 days or 1 week it would be better). How did you feel at the end of the first two days and how did you feel at the end of the last two days? Was there any difference? Write out what you noticed

_____

_____

_____

_____

_____

_____

_____

8. Your kids visit a relative for holidays and they were told it's wrong to play because it's a waste of time. They are almost convinced. What would you say to them?

_____

_____

_____

_____

_____

_____

_____

9. You're in charge of a group task at your work place. Look for ways to inculcate play in your task. Write out the task and how you'll bring play into it.

_____

_____

_____

_____

_____

_____

_____

10. Your boss finds out you've brought in play into work. He asks you how play will benefit work. You tell him work can't work without play and he asks you to explain. What would you say?

_____
_____
_____
_____
_____
_____
_____

11. What are the things you do when you want to rest and relax that bring you joy and accomplishment? Is it sleep, working out, going to see a movie, going to see friends, taking a nap, cooking or baking, spend time with loved ones? List them out

_____
_____
_____
_____
_____
_____
_____

12. What are the specific conditions you need for your rest and relax list? What can you do to put things in place? Is it taking a leave or having the weekend to yourself and your family? Mention them.

_____
_____
_____
_____

_____

_____

_____

13. Write out your dream list. This list is for the things you're working towards and you've always looked forward to having them as an accomplishment an acquisition. It could be taking a family vacation on any Caribbean island, buying a new house or touring on a yatch. List them out.

_____

_____

_____

_____

_____

_____

_____

14. Compare both lists. Which one gives you more peace without striving for anything? Which one makes your life simpler, fuller and yet joyful? Which should you give more of your attention?

_____

_____

_____

GUIDEPOST #8
Cultivating Calm and Stillness: LETTING GO OF ANXIETY AS A LIFESTYLE

Here are a few things we learned

- The best way to live an anxiety-free life is to cultivate calm and stillness and make it a lifestyle.
- A calm person can bring perspective to complicated situations and feel their feelings without reacting to heightened emotions like fear and anger. A panicked response produces more panic and more fear.
- In our complicated and anxious world we need more time to do less and be less.
- Practicing calmness and stillness may initially be difficult but as the practice becomes stronger, anxiety loses its hold and we gain clarity about what we're doing, where we are going and what holds true meaning for us.

Please answer the following questions as sincerely as you can

1. Calm is creating perspective and mindfulness while managing emotional reactivity.

   True [ ]

   False [ ]

2. Calmness is innate not practiced

   True [ ]

   False [ ]

3. Tick the boxes for the statements that are true

Anxiety is at an extreme of calm   [ ]

Anxiety is as contagious as calm   [ ]

Calmness involves a big pause before any decision is made   [ ]

Living with calm must be intentional and practiced   [ ]

Trying to practice stillness can make you jumpy   [ ]

Practicing calmness and stillness is pretty easy   [ ]

Stillness can make you over-function (takes control when anxious) [ ]

Anxiety can make you under-function (becomes less competent when anxious)   [ ]

4. Has there ever been a time you reacted emotionally to an issue and later found out your reaction was unnecessary?

Yes [ ]

No [ ]

i.   What happened?

_____

_____

_____

_____

_____

_____

_____

ii.   How did you feel afterwards?

_____

_____

_____

_____

_____

_____

_____

5. You visit your neighbor and you meet his wife angry because a friend told her she saw her husband smiling to another woman at the park and she left him there. (What she doesn't know is that it was her husband's sister). How can you help her calm down? Do you tell her to call him up, wait and verify details calmly or you tell her to get angry?

_____

_____

_____

_____

_____

_____

_____

6. Did you grow up in an environment where you saw people react out of anxiety or rage? If you did, do you think it affected you and how did you overcome it?

_____

_____

_____

_____

_____

_____

_____

7. What's the best way to train kids to calm down? Is it by shouting the words to them or acting it out? Write out your thoughts

_____

_____

_____

_____

_____

_____

_____

8. How can you practice calmness? Is it by sleeping well, eating well and reducing your caffeine? List out your strategies

_____

_____

_____

_____

_____

_____

_____

GUIDEPOST #9
Cultivating Meaningful Work:
LETTING GO OF SELF-DOUBT AND "SUPPOSED TO"

Here are a few things we learned

- Each individual has unique gifts and talents.
- Squandering our gifts brings distress, disconnection, frustration, emptiness, fear, disappointment shame and grief to our lives.
- Like gifts and talents, meaning is unique to each of us.
- Self-doubt undermines the process of finding our gifts and sharing them with the world. It is letting our fear undermine our faith.

Please answer the following questions as sincerely as you can

1. We struggle when we don't use our talents to cultivate meaningful work

True [ ]

False [ ]

2. Sharing our gifts and talents with the world is the most powerful source of connection with God

True [ ]

False [ ]

3. No one can define what's meaningful to you

True [ ]

False [ ]

4. Tick the boxes with the right statement

To live a Wholehearted life and engaging in meaningful work includes:

Anything that brings, joy, satisfaction and fulfillment [ ]

To share connection with others [ ]

To fit in [ ]

Anything involving hard work and sweat [ ]

Having gifts and talents [ ]

Having a good paying job [ ]

Staying committed [ ]

Having spirituality [ ]

    i.   Are there others? Mention them

_____

_____

_____

_____

_____

_____

_____

5. Does everyone have a gift and talent?

           Yes [ ]

           No [ ]

6. Do you think you have gifts and talents?

           Yes [ ]

           No [ ]

7. Your seven year old nephew has a gift of writing but he doesn't believe it. How do you convince him that his gift is enough or

important enough to be called a gift or talent? How do you convince him that he's enough?

_____

_____

_____

_____

_____

_____

_____

8. What would you call meaningful work? Is it dancing, sculpturing, singing or writing? Pen it down

_____

_____

_____

_____

_____

_____

_____

9. Is meaningful work a source of income for you? If your answer is no, why not? Is it time consuming or it can't pay the bills? Explain your reason why.

_____

_____

_____

_____

_____

_____

_____

10. Your teenage son has fashion skills but all his friends are into sports and they tease him about it so he feels he's not supposed to go into

fashion. How can you help him? Would you tell him to write out all his fears and address each one or would you tell him to be brave? Write out your plan

_____

_____

_____

_____

_____

_____

_____

11. Tick the boxes that best explain the purpose of gifts and talents

We derive fulfillment from our gifts and talents when we share them with the world   [ ]

Gifts and talents can only be groomed. We aren't born with it   [ ]

Gifts and talents help our spiritual connection   [ ]

Not using gifts and talents can make us ill   [ ]

Using gifts and talents gives us a sense of belonging   [ ]

Gifts and talents help us to find direction in life.   [ ]

GUIDEPOST #10
Cultivating Laughter, Song, and Dance: LETTING GO OF BEING COOL AND "ALWAYS IN CONTROL"

Here are a few lessons we learned in this chapter

- Laughter, song and dance are so woven into the fabric of our everyday life that we can forget how much we value the people who can make us laugh, the songs that inspire us to roll down the car window and sing at the top of our lungs, and the total freedom we feel when we dance like no one is watching.
- Laughter, song and dance create emotional and spiritual connection; they remind us of the one thing that truly matters when we are searching for comfort, celebration, inspiration or healing. We are not alone.
- Knowing laughter embodies the relief and connection we experience when we realize the power of sharing our stories. We're not laughing at each other but with each other.
- Songs have the ability to move us emotionally
- When we don't give ourselves permission to be free, we rarely tolerate that permission in others.

Please answer the following questions as sincerely as you can

1. Shame resilience requires laughter

    True [ ]

    False [ ]

2. Knowing laughter helps us heal

True [ ]

False [ ]

3. Tick the boxes that explain the purpose of laughter, song and dance

They help us as humans to express ourselves   [ ]

It helps us to be real within   [ ]

It helps us to share our narratives and experiences   [ ]

It helps us show emotions   [ ]

It helps us mourn, rejoice, and celebrate   [ ]

It helps us nurture community   [ ]

It makes life unbearable   [ ]

It's an essential part of our daily lives   [ ]

4. Has there ever been a time when you felt embarrassed but laughter helped you get over it?

Yes [ ]

No [ ]

5. Can you recall what happened?

_____
_____
_____
_____
_____
_____
_____

6. You face a bunch of children who are asking you questions randomly. One of them asks you why laughter, song and dance are important to them as children. What would you tell them?

_____
_____
_____
_____
_____
_____
_____

7. Have you ever frowned at someone who was dancing happily or singing so loud but happily in publicly?

Yes [ ]

No [ ]

8. Why? Was it too awkward? Explain your reason

_____
_____
_____
_____
_____
_____
_____

9. Have you ever tried to dance in public but you didn't? Why? Were you scared of being perceived as not cool or losing control? What were your reasons?

_____
_____
_____
_____

_____

_____

_____

10. One day when you get home after a long day and you feel drained or sad. Try to listen to good music and dance. Make sure you dance with all that you feel. Note how you feel before you start dancing and how you feel afterwards. Write it down.

_____

_____

_____

_____

_____

_____

_____

11. Create dance nights or sing-a-long nights for you and your family. Be happy and forget about staying in control as you do it.

Made in the USA
Middletown, DE
07 August 2021